EMERALD
4502 ~~~~ ~~~ SW
Seattle, WA 98116

MW00856256

TROUT FLIES
& FLOWERS

EASTERN

—◆—

IVAN L. MAHONEY

ILLUSTRATED BY
VEVA CROZER

LUKKEN COLOR

Published in the United States of America

10 9 8 7 6 5 4 3 2 1

Library of Congress Cataloging-in-Publication Data applied for.

Printed in Canada   ISBN 1-55821-72

To Beth and George with love.

ACKNOWLEDGMENTS

A very special thank you is deserved by the people, who so importantly helped us turn this pile of ideas into a book. To Eldridge Arnold, who took us both to the stream and Peggy Arnold for encouragement on the drawings. Frank Kuttner for tying, in the Catskill tradition, all the flies illustrated, and Ed Lundquist, a true master of the stream, for so generously sharing his immense knowledge. Also Marian Young, for leading us through the caverns of the publishing business. And Marie Coons, of Mada Design, for the beautiful layout. Allen Green for the "snap" on the back cover, and sending us to Mada Design. Donna Warner for support and a great recipe. And Leigh Perkins for his encouragement to chase an idea.

PREFACE

A few years ago I was invited by a good friend to try fly fishing for trout after a long hiatus. I remember being fortunate enough to catch a few fish, but I don't recall the names of the flies that we used that day. In fact, my most vivid memory of the day was a clump of Blue Flag Iris that was blooming by the side of the dirt road we followed to reach the pool we were to fish.

That clump of Iris started me thinking. Later with my fishing partner, an avid gardener capable of identifying the plants blooming stream-side, and my limited knowledge of the insects that were hatching at the time, we soon discovered that the blooming period of certain plants coincided with the hatches of specific insects. Once we became aware of the connection our fishing improved dramatically.

This book has been put together for one specific purpose— to help you choose the fly that best represents the insect hatching in the stream. While there are charts that indicate what is going to happen hatch-wise each year, they can be weeks off as we all know. Unlike most fly fishers, biological events are not bound by the Julian calendar. Plant and insect life cycles are governed by their environmental surroundings and respond to an abstract calendar that does not necessarily follow our man-made version.

For the purposes of this book it is unnecessary to discuss and understand the science that is responsible for what is occurring in and near the trout stream. There are many fine scientific publications, should you be so inclined, that explain in detail what is being graphically presented here. With this system, you only need to stop, smell and, most importantly, see the flowers for a moment. Then enjoy the fishing.

The illustrations, which my fishing partner has created, are not true botanical drawings but are portraits of flowers. If a leaf was growing in front of the blossom, it was removed so that we could make the plant easier to identify.

We have not illustrated all the plants mentioned in this book. You may want to consider purchasing one of the excellent comprehensive field guides that are available. If possible try to find one with colored illustrations.

The fly illustrations are of the traditional Catskill tie and color, which have evolved over the years into the current accepted representations.

TROUT FLIES
& FLOWERS

INTRODUCTION

This book answers the most frequently asked question in fly fishing: "What fly should I use?"

In the past, you had to have a knowledge of entomology and Latin to identify the insect hatching in the stream, then convert the Latin, or proper name, to the English, or common name, which you could then match to the fly. Well, you get the picture. Alternatively, you could use the "this worked last time" or the "this looks delicious" method, but you will invariably come to the same conclusion: there must be a better way. And there is.

This book illustrates graphically what fly pattern to fish with, where to use it on the stream, the most productive time of day and also what size fly to use. This book will teach you how to relate the fly pattern to the plants, trees and shrubs that are blooming or leafing out in the area that you are planning to fish. For our purposes we will concentrate only on the insects that make for good trout fishing, and the indicator-plants that can tell us when the sport will be at its best.

The major tree and plant indicators are represented by a graphic illustration, the common, English name, and, because fly fishing possesses a rich tradition, the Latin, or proper name.

I think that you will find it much less difficult to recognize Forsythia, a bright yellow, bushy shrub, standing six to eight feet tall, than an inch long March Brown Mayfly hatching in the stream. They are both telling us to tie on a March Brown and enjoy some of the best large fly fishing of the season.

To use this book, first recognize and match a plant illustrated or referenced within these pages to one you see near the stream. Then check the water condition and the stream location keys for the appropriate place in the stream for the hatch to occur. Next, tie on the fly in the suggested size, and have fun. Even if the fishing is slow, you will know that the fly chosen was the proper one to start with and that you are working out of the correct corner of your fly box. And if the sport is really good you will have discovered it much sooner than if you had been using one of the hit-or-miss methods of old.

wood duck feather

THEN & NOW

"Except to a studious few, dissertations upon the intricacies of Entomology and the artificial fly nomenclature are worrysome and to be avoided."

Mary Orvis Marbury, 1982
Favorite Flies and their History

"I might tell you of many more, which as these doe early, so those have their time turning to be flies later in the summer; but I may lose myself and tire you of my discourse."

Izaak Walton on Caddis flies, 1653
The Compleat Angler

The above quotes show that starting fly fishing can be as intimidating and confusing as a blind date. The arrangements for both are complicated, the clothing for a date is at least as difficult to organize as the gear for your first trip to a trout stream.

Everyone who picks up a fly rod and heads for the stream wants to appear as if he belongs there. Gear shouldn't be too new and clothes not too old, a modest casting ability would help. (Don't even think of catching anything.)

The next desire is to catch a fish. Any fish. And then to catch a limit, which would require a deal with the Fishing Spirit, the unknown and powerful force that makes you fish to excess and buy equipment that you don't need.

And then, to be able to hook into THE BIG ONE, the fish of a lifetime, a twenty-inch plus brown, on a size 20 Adams with a 7X leader and tippet. The three weight rod is maxed out, the fish rolls in the shallows. You see it.

Huge! What do you do now? (Say good-bye, you should have walked the fish down to the next pool. But don't worry you'll get the same chance in a few years more years.)

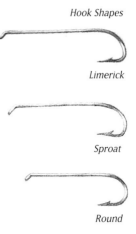

Hook Shapes

Limerick

Sproat

Round

FLOWERS & FLIES

In the spring when the ground warms, seeds germinate, bulbs come to life, and trees leaf out and flower. The same activity is taking place in the trout stream, but it is much less obvious to us. The same major factors, heat and light, are the stimulant for both the soil and stream activity. The insects, the major source of the trout diet, are simultaneously entering this vitally important reproductive period.

Just as we know that plants and trees bloom and leaf out in a specific order (surely you have seen the Crocus before the Daffodils before the Tulips before the Lilacs), insects hatches occur in the same order as well, Quill Gordons before the Hendricksons before the March Browns before the Green Drakes. By observing what is growing and blooming stream-side, you will be able to determine what is occurring hatch-wise in the stream. You may have to fine tune the information for the area you are going to be fishing, but the results will be the same. You will be able to zero in on what is hatching and which fly to fish with.

Refer to a hardiness zone chart as a rough guide of what to expect to see blooming in the area you plan to fish. Hardiness charts are available in seed catalogs and at garden supply stores. You can also contact a local nursery near the streams you intend to visit and ask them when the referenced plants will bloom. Be sure to remember that altitude reduces temperature and slows blooming and hatches. The fly fisherman's "hatches move upstream" pronouncement is explained by these small altitude changes.

The drawings and graphic representations of stream condition and water level are designed to help to determine the portion of the stream where and when a fly can be used most effectively. Remember, certain insects hatch in different places in the stream. This is graphically indicated in the Legend of this book.

LEGEND

The drawings in this book are categorized three different ways.

The first category is the plant drawings. Cultivated or introduced plants have been chosen when possible because they are often easier to find. Naturally occurring species which are easily recognized are also illustrated.

The second group is indicated by rectangles with waves. This represents the water conditions.

The drawings in the third category are the flies which represent the insect hatches that occur when the illustrated plant blooms.

The illustrations reference both the English, common name, and the Latin, proper name, of each subject plant. The English and Latin names are also listed for the insect hatches. The purpose of listing both names is to avoid confusion. The same plant may have a different name in another part of the country. The same may also be true with fly pattern names.

The early indicator plants may be difficult to find as there are fewer of them, or may not yet be blooming when you make your first trips to the stream. A call to the nursery or garden supply center in the area you plan to visit can be one of the simplest ways to determine what is blooming and thus hatching.

WATER CONDITIONS

 LOW WATER

 HIGH

 OPTIMUM

 ALL TYPES

LOCATION

 SLOW WATER

 FAST WATER

 RIFFLE

 ALL TYPES

ANDROMEDA

Andromeda is an evergreen, bushy shrub that grows to a height of eight feet. The flowers appear in drooping clusters either white or white with a touch of pink. Andromeda is a cultivated plant. Look for it in gardens or as foundation planting.

Also look for:
- Pussy Willows in wetlands
- Snow Drops
- Skunk cabbage whorls in swamps and wetlands

⇒◆⇐

A "cast" is the Old English discription of the flies tied leader, usually two or more. Today "cast" has become a verb.

⇒◆⇐

Try a cast of a #12 Bead Head above a #6 Wolly Bugger if the water is above optimum condition.

The Stone dry fly should be best in the afternoon, the nymph and streamer anytime.

NOTES: _____

_____

_____

_____

_____

ANDROMEDA

(Pieris japonica)

WATER

LOCATION

BROWN STONE FLY
(Tainioperytx fasciata)

BROWN STONE FLY
dry #10-#16

WOLLEY BUGGER
wet #6-#12

BEAD HEAD
nymph #10-#16

GLORY OF THE SNOW

The Glory of the Snow is an early spring flowering bulb that sometimes blooms before the snow has melted. A rich blue-lilac colored flower with white eyes and two semi-erect leaves. Naturalizes easily and can be found in new or abandoned gardens. Height 4 to 10 inches.

Also look for:
- Myrtle
- Early Daffodils
- Maple trees just beginning to show red

The Quill Gordon is the first major dry fly fishing of the season. Look for the hatch to start about 1:30.

Myrtle

NOTES: _____

_____

_____

_____

_____

GLORY OF THE SNOW

(Chionodoxa forbsii)

WATER

LOCATION

QUILL GORDON
(Epeorus pleuralis/Iron fraudator)

QUILL GORDON
dry #12-#14

GOLD BAND HARE'S EAR
nymph #12-#14

IRON NYMPH
nymph #12-#14

FORSYTHIA

Forsythia is a graceful, arching shrub with bright yellow flowers that appear before the leaves. Height to 8 feet.

Also look for:
■ Pansies
■ Dutchman's Britches

The Blue Quill hatches are mostly midday. Smaller flies usually are more productive during this hatch.

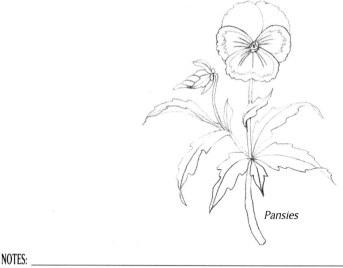

Pansies

NOTES: _____

_____

_____

_____

_____

FORSYTHIA
(Forsythia suspensa)

WATER

LOCATION

BLUE QUILL
(Paraleptophlebia adoptiva)

BLUE QUILL
dry #18-#20

BLUE QUILL
wet #16-#18

LEPTOPHLEBIA
nymph #16-#18

VIOLETS

The violet blooms in the early spring, the leaf stalks are often longer than the flower stalks.

Also look for:
- Flowering Pear
- Colts Foot, a yellow dandelion like flower with no leaves
- Wild Cherry trees budding
- Primrose

The Hendrickson is known for the two dry fly patterns associated with the hatch. The Red Quill in size 14 represents the male, and the female is represented by the Hendrickson on a size 12 hook. The Hendrickson is easier to see, being of a lighter color, but the Red Quill is equally important, alternate between the two.

⇒◆⇐

The dry action starts at 2:00 in the afternoon, rain or shine according to Ed Lundquist, a well respected Beaverkill Pro.

⇒◆⇐

Listen for Wild Turkeys gobbling in the early morning.

NOTES: _____

_____

_____

_____

Flowering Pear

4

VIOLETS
(Viola orderata)

WATER

LOCATION

HENDRICKSON
(Ephemerella subvaria)

HENDRICKSON
dry #12-#14

RED QUILL
dry #12-#14

RUSTY
spinner #14

WAKE ROBIN

Trillium, with its purple or red flower is easily spotted in the woods of early trout season. The flower is on a short stalk, growing between 8 and 16 inches in height.

The Shad run in the rivers when the Shadbush is blooming. Shad are great sport on a fly rod.

Also look for:
■ Bloodroot
■ Garlic Mustard

The March Brown hatches occur sporadically throughout the day in most areas of the stream. Nymphs and Spinners will be most productive in the faster water.

March Brown

NOTES: _____

_____

_____

_____

_____

5

WAKE ROBIN

(Trillium erectum)

WATER

LOCATION

MARCH BROWN
(Stenonema vicarium)

MARCH BROWN
dry #10–#12

STENONEMA
nymph #10–#12

RUSTY
spinner #12

DOGWOOD

The Dogwood is a May flowering tree, with white or pink-ish white flowers. The trees are usually as wide or wider than they are tall. They are found at the edge of the woods.

Also look for:
- Forget-me-nots
- Crab Apple
- Lily-of-the-Valley

Watch out for Poison Ivy; leaves are just coming out.

The Sulphur are one of the most consistent and longest occurring hatches, when in doubt of what to use at dusk try a sulphur.

Sulpher Dun

NOTES: _____

_____

_____

_____

_____

6

DOGWOOD
(Cornus florida)

WATER

LOCATION

SULPHER DUN
(Epeorus vitrea/Ephemerella dorothea)

SULPHER
dry #14-#18

EPHEMERELLA
nymph #14-#18

SULPHER
spinner #16-#18

HONEYSUCKLE

These Honeysuckle flowers are two inches long, yellow-ish-white, and the bush can grow to twenty feet in height.

Also look for:
- Dames Rocket; varied in color white, pink or purple, height 1-3 feet
- Lilac
- Azaleas

———◆———

The blooming of flowers has long been used to mark historic as well as biological events, as evidenced by Poet Walt Whitman's remembrance of the death of Abraham Lincoln with the great When Lilacs Last in the Dooryard Bloom'd.

———◆———

The Gray Fox is another hatch that can be sporadic in timing, if you should be fishing faster water try the nymph or the spinner.

NOTES: _____

_____

_____

_____

_____

7

HONEYSUCKLE

(Lonicera)

WATER

LOCATION

GREY FOX
(Stenonema fuscum)

GREY FOX
dry #12-#14

STENONEMA
nymph #12

GINGER
spinner #12-#14

SOLOMAN'S SEAL

Solomon's Seal has paired yellow flowers that dangle from the base of the leaves, found in woods and thickets.

Also look for:
- Horsechestnut trees blooming
- Wild geranium flowering along roadsides. This is also known as cranesbill, because the fruit develop a beak like shape.

The Dun Variants hatch late in the day in the fast water sections of the stream.

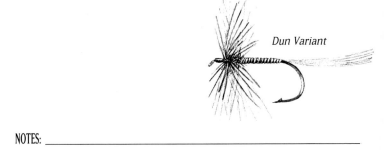

Dun Variant

NOTES: _____

_____

_____

_____

_____

8

SOLOMAN'S SEAL
(Polygonatum biflorum)

WATER

LOCATION

DUN VARIANT
(Isonychia bicolor)

DUN VARIANT
dry #10-#14

ISONYCHIA
nymph #10-#14

LIGHT GREY
spinner #10-#12

BEARDED IRIS

The Iris illustrated is a cultivated variety that is available in many colors all with a strong gold beard. The larger Blue Flag Iris is wild and blooms in wet areas.

Also look for:
- Indian Strawberries
- Cedar Waxwings return and start nest building.

The Green Drake hatches usually afford the best large fly action of the season. The large white colored spinner, or coffin fly, is easily seen during the evening rise.

Coral Bells

NOTES: _____

_____

_____

_____

_____

9

BEARDED IRIS

(Iris germanica)

WATER

LOCATION

GREEN DRAKE
(Ephemera guttulata)

GREEN DRAKE
dry #10–#12

DARK EPHEMERA
nymph #8–#12

COFFIN FLY
spinner #10

MAPLE SPINNER

Look for the light green spinners amidst the darker green leaves of this Maple.

Also look for:
- Wild Roses.
- Peonies in gardens or around abandoned farms.
- Tulip Poplar; look for the yellow blooms at the ends of the tree's branches.

Cahill hatches occurr sporadically, the evening spinner fall can provide fast action.

The Light Cahill means the large fly season is nearing an end, so plan an extra day if you can. Ed Lundquist suggests a size 12 Cahill with a size 18 Sulphur dry as a dropper if the fishing slows during the day. Try a spinner in the fast water at dusk.

Wild Rose

NOTES: _____

_____

_____

_____

_____

10

MAPLE SPINNER
(Acer platanoides)

WATER

LOCATION

LIGHT CAHILL
(Stenonema canadense)

LIGHT CAHILL
dry #12–#14

STENONEMA
nymph #12–#14

RUSTY
spinner #14

SWEET PEAS

The Sweet Pea illustrated is the common garden variety and comes in many colors. The wild Everlasting Sweet Pea is a garden escapee and blooms at the same time.

Also look for:
- Mountain Laurel
- Fox Glove
- Climbing Hydrangea

Blue Wing Olive hatches can start at any time, although the fly is small and dark, try it when nothing else is working.

The smaller dark flies are difficult to see at times, so pick a bubble or something floating on the water near the fly. If there is a rise near the bubble, lift the rod tip, you may be pleasantly surprised.

Mountain Laurel

NOTES: _____

_____

_____

_____

_____

SWEET PEAS

(Lathyrus odoratus)

WATER

LOCATION

BLUE WING OLIVE
(Ephemerella attenuata)

BLUE WING OLIVE
dry #14-#16

EPHEMERELLA
nymph #14-#16

BLUE QUILL
spinner #14-#16

ASTILBE

Astilbe blooms in white, pink, or reds from 2 to 3 feet in height. The lighter colors generally bloom before the darker reds.

Also look for:
- Wild Garlic
- Wild Onion
- Cultivated Lilies
- Beardtongue foxglove
- Fairy Roses

Look for the Cream Variant in the evening in slower water, the Spinner fall occurs in faster water.

At this time of the fishing season the water levels can be high. A streamer, wet fly, or nymph that is fished deep or close to the bottom can be successful.

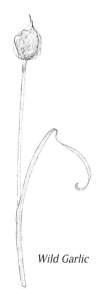

Wild Garlic

NOTES: _____

_____

_____

_____

_____

ASTILBE
(Astilbe "Venus")

WATER

LOCATION

CREAM VARIANT
(Ephemera varia)

CREAM VARIANT
dry #12-#14

EPHEMERA
nymph #10-#12

YELLOW DRAKE
spinner #12

12

DAY LILIES

Daylillies require a lot of sun to bloom so be sure to pick a sunny exposure when checking for flowers. We have seen plants that rarely bloom because they don't receive enough light.

Also look for:
- Hollyhocks
- Rhododendron maximum
- Bindweed
- Privet
- Queen Anne's Lace

Caddis hatches can be plentiful and long lasting at most times of the day. A caddis can be fished both wet and dry, try sinking the fly at the end of the drift.

Hollyhock

NOTES: _____

_____

_____

_____

_____

13

DAY LILIES
(*Hemerocallis fulva*)

WATER

LOCATION

CADDIS FLIES
(Hyrdopsyche/Helicopsyche)

ELK HAIR CADDIS
dry or wet #16-#22

DAVE'S HOPPER
dry or wet #16-#22

HENRYVILLE SPECIAL
dry or wet #16-#22

BLACK-EYED SUSAN

Black-eyed Susans grow in fields and waste areas from Nova Scotia south. They are three feet tall and one of the most recognizable flowers on the roadside during the summer.

Also look for:
- Creeping Bellflowers
- Purple Cone Flowers
- Mullein
- Purple Loosetrife— Hopefully we will see less of this import, it is displacing our naturally occurring wetland plants.

Tricos are usually visible at most times of the day in the sun light over riffles, and should be fished wet or dry.

Creeping Bellflower

NOTES: _____

_____

_____

_____

_____

14

BLACK-EYED SUSAN
(Rudbeckia hirta)

WATER

LOCATION

TRICO
(Trocorythodes sp.)

TRICO
dry or wet #12-#26

BLACK ANT
dry or wet #12-#26

BEETLE
dry or wet #12-#26

SPOTTED JOE-PYE-WEED

Flowers are dull pinkish purple, with deep purple or purple spotted stems. Height is from 2 to 7 ft. growing in wet thickets and meadows from Canada to the southern mountains.

Also look for:
- Butterfly Weed
- Horse Nettles
- Goldenrod
- Knotweed

Listen for Cicadas.

This is the time of the season to use the small flies. Midges, Parachute Adams, and small Olives, ants and other terrestrials.

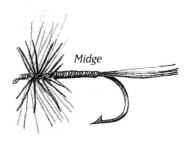
Midge

NOTES: _____

_____

_____

_____

_____

SPOTTED JOE-PYE-WEED

(Eupatorium maculatum)

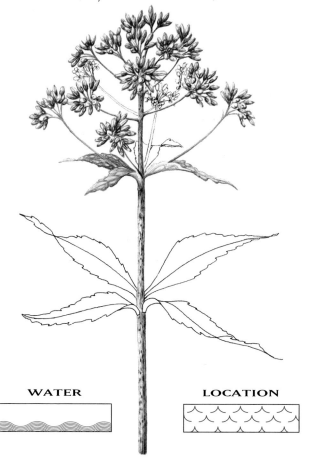

WATER

LOCATION

MIDGE
(Chironomus)

MIDGE
#18-#22

PARACHUTE ADAMS
#18-#22

OLIVE PARACHUTE
#22

OLD FAVORITES

The flies illustrated are responsible for a share of trout caught in this country. The reason is two fold, the first, and most obvious reason is name recognition, the second is they work!

Streamers are often the patterns to try when nothing else is working. Over seventy five percent of the trout diet consists of subsurface food. Streamers are large and offer a good swimming motion, which is thought to simulate the maximum food value for effort expended by the fish.

The Prince Nymph is one of the most used nymphs. The name is easy to remember and is found in most nymph boxes. A small prince is usually the dropper of choice.

The Dry flies shown are all attractor patterns. Attractors are not imitations of actual insects, but these flies can catch fish. The Adams is considered to be the most used trout fly, everyone has a few in their box because the name is quickly recalled. The Royal Wulff is probably the most used fly at dusk because it is easy to see in low light conditions. The other flies are not as name recognizable, or as common in every fly box but they also can be productive.

The most important part of fly selection is to have fun fishing. Some days that means changing flies too quickly, and on another day not changing a fly, so enjoy your time on the stream.

OLD FAVORITES

MICKEY FINN

MUDDLER

BLACK NOSED DACE

MATUKA

PRINCE NYMPH

ADAMS

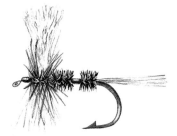

ROYAL WULFF

KATTERMANN

THOUGHTS & PRESENTATION

I have often wondered if thinking about how to get a trout to take your fly is actually as much fun as doing it. The answer is elusive, and probably changes with the phases of one's life.

When I had my first fly casting lesson some years ago, it was not a pleasant experience. I was on the front lawn with my father, a very capable caster, attempting to develop any technique I could manage. My frustration was unfortunately exceeded only by his disappointment. At the end of the lesson, I decided that fly fishing was for the other guys.

Some years later, when I took another look at the sport, I began to notice what I had missed. I enthusiastically managed to teach myself to cast, and present a fly with a proper drift both up stream and down stream. I learned to make long casts very well, but not the more important shorter ones. I thought I looked great — I was ready for one of those Saturday morning TV shows. I knew that my presentation was acceptable, but I really didn't know how to take full advantage of it, and wasn't as successful in the stream as I should have been.

After a few sessions with the Pro, who did such a wonderful job of teaching the kids to fly fish, I was able to shake most of the self-taught bad habits I had developed over the years. But more importantly, I started to notice what was happening on and in the water. I also learned that kids learned easier from pros than they do generally from parents.

The proper presentation of the correct fly will give you the chance to catch a fish on each cast. You may not, but you should always be prepared for it. Many fish are missed because of pilot error, be it the frustration of not setting the hook quickly enough when the trout rises to the fly, or the mistake of letting the fly drag in the current and leave a wake (Would you eat something that was leaving a wake on your soup? Trout won't either).

The most elegant bamboo rod with the perfectly matched reel won't catch any extra fish without time spent with the fly in the water.

Fortunately it appears that catch and release is here to stay, but don't feel badly if you keep a few for the table, and if you choose to do so, try the recipe on page 50. And if you enjoy classical music try some of Schubert's Trout Music.

FLY BOX SET UP

Each Christmas for the past few years Beth, my daughter, visited the local fly shop to buy George, my stepson, his ration of flies. The salesman would ask what flies she wanted, and she would answer, "Doesn't matter." Well, where do you think he will be fishing? "Doesn't matter," was the same perplexing response. The salesman, suffering from holiday season burn-out would insist that it really does matter, to which Beth would invariably reply, "Well, we fish on the Beaverkill most of the time, but it really doesn't matter. He is going to lose most of them, and the ones he doesn't lose I will borrow from him and lose myself."

When Christmas is over and done, and the doldrums of winter setting in, the need to organize and prepare becomes apparent. But how to organize, and what to prepare? In our family, whenever one of us figures out that he or she (ninety nine percent of the time it is one of the shes!) has lost perspective on one thing or another an organizational moment cannot by far away. The fly boxes are always the first order of business. Witness the birth of the science of Fly Inventory management (FIM).

As George was wondering aloud, "I have all these flies from Christmas. How do you think I should set up my fly box? After all the fishing season is only three or four months away."

I am certainly not be the wisest man on earth, but I know better than to give a direct answer to a question about something as personal as a fly box, clothing, or a girlfriend. Being quite impressed with myself, I responded with a question I already knew the answer to: "What hatches first, and why not set up your box in the order of the hatches?'

Unfortunately, I left myself wide open. George thought about it for a moment, then said, "That's a great way to do it, but I'll need a few more boxes and can I have that big water-proof one you're only partly using also the small aluminum box that you use for nymphs?"

Wheatly, my best small British fly box, and I had been friends for many years, but off he went to his new home, with the provision I could borrow the box back. I was actually impressed with myself for getting away for only a fly box: I once lost my 4-wheel drive to my daughter for a whole winter semester, a "safety" thing, as I recall.

I, like nature, abhor a vacuum. The empty pocket in my fish-ing vest that was formerly occupied by my favorite fly box was a cause for major concern. I cleared my desk, pulled out the fishing catalogs, and made myself a martini on the rocks to put me in sync with the gin-clear, icy, January trout streams, to give this FIM problem some thought.

In the past I arranged my flies chronologically, i.e. in the order that I bought them. When one box filled up, I would go and buy another one. A full, bulging fishing vest made me look like a pro, but in all honesty I didn't know what was in it, or where to find things. A fishing friend tried to set me straight by pointing out that my fly boxes were a mess. When I asked him how he orga-nized his boxes, he said, "Alphabetically." I knew even then that "alphabetically" wasn't the answer, because I knew he made up his own names for his flies. What really frosted him was my ask-ing him whether he alphabetized in English or Latin.

I made a pest of myself and asked everyone I knew how they kept order in their fly boxes. The only constant, I discovered, was the total lack of consistency in the answers. Some arranged by nymphs, wets, streamers, and dries, or dry and wet of the same pattern together, or whatever. Others arranged by the stream they intended to fish, or by the rate of success they had with a fly previously. Obviously, the fly box arrangement that works best is the one that you best understand, but at this point, my idea of organizing a fly box by the order in which the insects hatch began to look very good. I am now convinced that this organization method is the most practical solution, as it mirrors what is happening in the stream.

Since the indicator flowers bloom in a specific order, and that shows you what is hatching in the stream, why not set up your boxes by the number in the hatch order, or by the numbers on the Bloom/Hatch chart on page 46 you will notice a number associated with each plant and fly referenced. This is the same number that is indicated in the color code on the plant illustration pages. The numbers tell you the order in which plants bloom and the insects hatch. I use these numbers to set up my fly boxes. I keep the dry, wet, nymph, and spinner of each fly pattern under the same number. This arrangement allows me to fish a pattern completely before trying another. The set up removes the temptation of fishing with a fly that should be used in August in May.

During the first part of the season there are fewer plants blooming and insects hatches at the same time. Later in the season, as the days get longer and warmer there are more hatches occurring in a shorter period of time. If there are multiple hatches occurring in the stream, you can easily bracket the fly pattern if you have your boxes organized by hatch order, just as a photographer would bracket for over and under exposure. Try the pattern that hatches before or after the one you have been using. The plant indicators will tell you what to start with, and keep you fishing out of he right corner of your fly box.

FLY/FLOWER CHART

	COMMON NAME	PROPER NAME
#1		
Plant	ANDROMEDA	(Pieris japonica)
Pattern	BROWN STONE FLY	(Taenioperytx fasciata)
Dry #10-16	Wet #6-12	Nymph #10-16
Brown stone	Wolly Bugger	Bead Nymph
#2		
Plant	GLORY OF THE SNOW	(Chionodoxa forbsii)
Pattern	QUILL GORDON	(Epeorus pleuralis/Iron fraudator)
Dry #12-14	Wet #12-14	Nymph #12-14 Spinner #14
Quill Gordon	Hare's Ear	Iron Nymph Red Quill
#3		
Plant	FORSYTHIA	(Forsythia suspensa)
Pattern	BLUE QUILL	(Paraleptophlebia adoptiva)
	DARK BLUE QUILL	(Baetis sp.)
Dry #18-20	Wet #16-18	Nymph #16-18 Spinner #18
Blue Quill	Blue Quill	Leptophlebia Dark Quill
#4		
Plant	VIOLETS	(Viola)
Pattern	HENDRICKSON	(Ephemerella subvaria)
Dry #12-14	Wet #12-14	Nymph #12-14 Spinner #14
Hendrickson	Hare's ear	Ephemerella Rusty
#5		
Plant	WAKE ROBIN	(Trillium erectum)
Pattern	MARCH BROWN	(Stenonema vicarium)
Dry #10-12	Nymph #10-12	Spinner #12
March Brown		Stenonema Red
#6		
Plant	DOGWOOD	(Cornus florida)
Pattern	SULPHER DUN	(Epeorus vitrea/
		Ephemerella dorothea)
Dry #14-18	Wet #14-18	Nymph #14-18 Spinner #16-18
Sulpher	Sulpher	Ephemerella Sulpher
#7		
Plant	HONEYSUCKLE	(Lonicera)
Pattern	GREY FOX	(Stenonema fuscum)
Dry #12=14	Wet #12-14	Nymph #12 Spinner #12-14
Grey Fox	Sunken dry	Stenonema Ginger

COMMON NAME		PROPER NAME	
#8			
Plant	SOLOMAN'S SEAL	(Polygonatum biflorum)	
Pattern	DUN VARIANT	(Isonychia bicolor)	
Dry #10-14	Wet	Nymph #10-14	Spinner #10-12
Dun Variant	none	Isonychia	Light Grey
#9			
Plant	BEARDED IRIS	(Iriis germanica)	
Pattern	GREEN DRAKE	(Ephemera guttulata)	
Dry #10-12	Wet	Nymph #8-12	Spinner #10
Green Drake	none	Dark Ephemera	Coffin Fly
#10			
Plant	MAPLE SPINNER	(Acer platanoides)	
Pattern	LIGHT CAHILL	(Stenonema canadense)	
Dry	Wet	Nymph #12-14	Spinner #14
Light Cahill	#12-14	Stenonema	Rusty
#11			
Plant	SWEET PEAS	(Lathyrus odoratus)	
Pattern	BLUE WING OLIVE	(Ephemerella attenuata)	
Dry #14-16	Wet	Nymph #14-16	Spinner #14-16
Blue Wing Olive	none	Ephemerella	Blue Quill
#12			
Plant	ASTILBE	(Astilbe "Venus")	
Pattern	CREAM VARIANT	(Ephemera varia)	
Dry	Wet	Nymph #10-12	Spinner # 12
Cream Variant	#12-14	Ephemera	Yellow Drake
#13			
Plant	DAY LILLIES	(Hemerocallis fulva)	
Pattern	CADDIS FLIES	(Hyrdopsyche/Helicopsyche)	
	#16-22	Fished Dry or Wet	
#14			
Plant	BLACK-EYED SUSAN	(Rudbeckia hirta)	
Pattern	TRICO	(Trocorythodes sp.)	
	#22-26	Fished Dry or Wet	
#15			
Plant	SPOTTED JOE-PYE-WEED	(Eupatorium maculatum)	
Pattern	MIDGE	(Chironomus)	
	#18-22	Fished Dry or Wet	

TROUT DONNA-DONNA

Although I am practitioner of catch and release, and return all but a few of the fish I have hooked each year, I am not all that disappointed when a dinner or lunch of Trout Donna-Donna is in the offing. The fish that I keep for table fare are usually unable to be returned to the water because they have been injured, or are exhausted and have not responded to attempts to revive them. I find it quite unpleasant to gaze into the stream and see a fish belly up at the bottom of a pool and much prefer the vision of the same fish on a plate. Should you land a fish that is bleeding or one that repeatedly refuses to swim away dispatch it quickly. This fish is the responsibility of anyone who picks up a fly rod.

The recipe is inspired by the chef at Restaurant Leslie, who served it many years ago in New York, however its roots are very French. The recipe was given to us by Donna Warner, Editor in Chief, of Metropolitan Home Magazine, thus the name.

Sautéed Trout with Bacon

8 slices of bacon
freshly ground pepper
4 trout cleaned, with head and tail left on
(about 3/4 to 1 lb. each)
2 shallots, pealed and sliced
4 bay leaves, fresh if possible
1 cup good, dry red wine

Fry the bacon slices in a large, heavy skillet. When brown, remove and drain on paper towels. Crumble into 1/2 " pieces and set aside. Pour out and discard all but about two tablespoons of the bacon fat.

Pat trout dry with paper towels and pepper to taste. Turn the heat under the skillet to medium high and add the trout. Cook about 5 minutes a side, (the classic fish cooking rule is 10 minutes for every inch of thickness) or until crispy and brown.

Remove trout to warm dinner plates. Add shallots and bay leaves and sauté quickly over medium heat until shallots are transparent. Add red wine, stir to scrape up all the delicious brown bits, and simmer to reduce by half. Pour the sauce over the fish, add crumbled bacon and serve immediately.

Serve with dry red wine

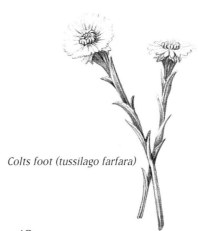

Colts foot (tussilago farfara)

BROWN STONE FLY

QUILL GORDON

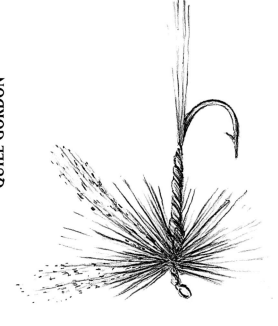

DATE   PLANT   FLY   STREAM

BLUE QUILL

DATE   PLANT   FLY   STREAM

HENDRICKSON

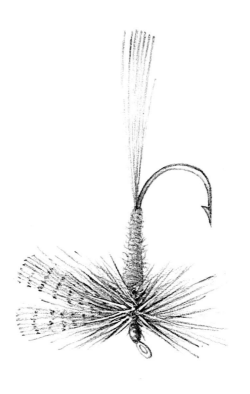

DATE   PLANT   FLY   STREAM

MARCH BROWN

DATE   PLANT   FLY   STREAM

SULPHUR

GREY FOX

DATE   PLANT   FLY   STREAM

DUN VARIANT

GREEN DRAKE

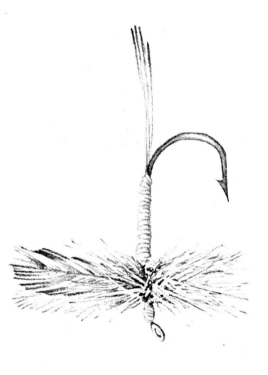

LIGHT CAHILL

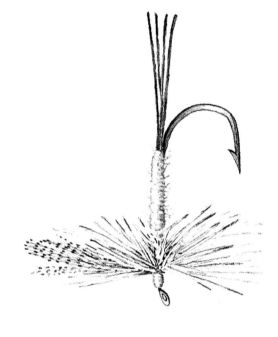

BLUE WING OLIVE

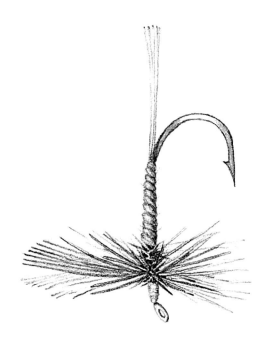

DATE　　　　　　　　PLANT　　　　　　　　FLY　　　　　　　　STREAM

CREAM VARIANT

CADDIS

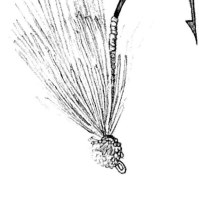

DATE   PLANT   FLY   STREAM

TRICO

DATE   PLANT   FLY   STREAM

MIDGE

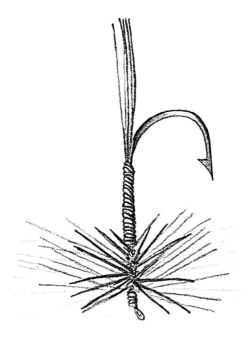

DATE   PLANT   FLY   STREAM